THE WALLABY WITH WILLPOWER

A CHILDREN'S BOOK ABOUT DECIDING HOW TO SPEND MONEY, KNOWING HOW TO PLAN FOR THE FUTURE, AND KEEPING YOUR FINANCIAL PRIORITIES STRAIGHT

WRITTEN BY CHARLOTTE DANE

ILLUSTRATED BY ADAM RIONG

However, pizzas were expensive, and Wallaby knew it would mean he couldn't afford dinner in the future - the next day.
So Mama Wallaby's lasagna it was!

For instance, one time, Wallaby saw an action figure of his favorite childhood heroes. Awesome! He bought them without a second thought.

The problem was that Wallaby often forgot that he would need money later on. If not that same day, then the next day, or over the weekend.

One day, Wallaby's friend Fox saw him sitting at a table with a huge amount of food! Every type of food was there, and every dessert too.

Fox understood. He saw that Wallaby had an issue with planning for the future, and what he might need his money for in the future. So he took him to the mirror house in a carnival to demonstrate for him more clearly.

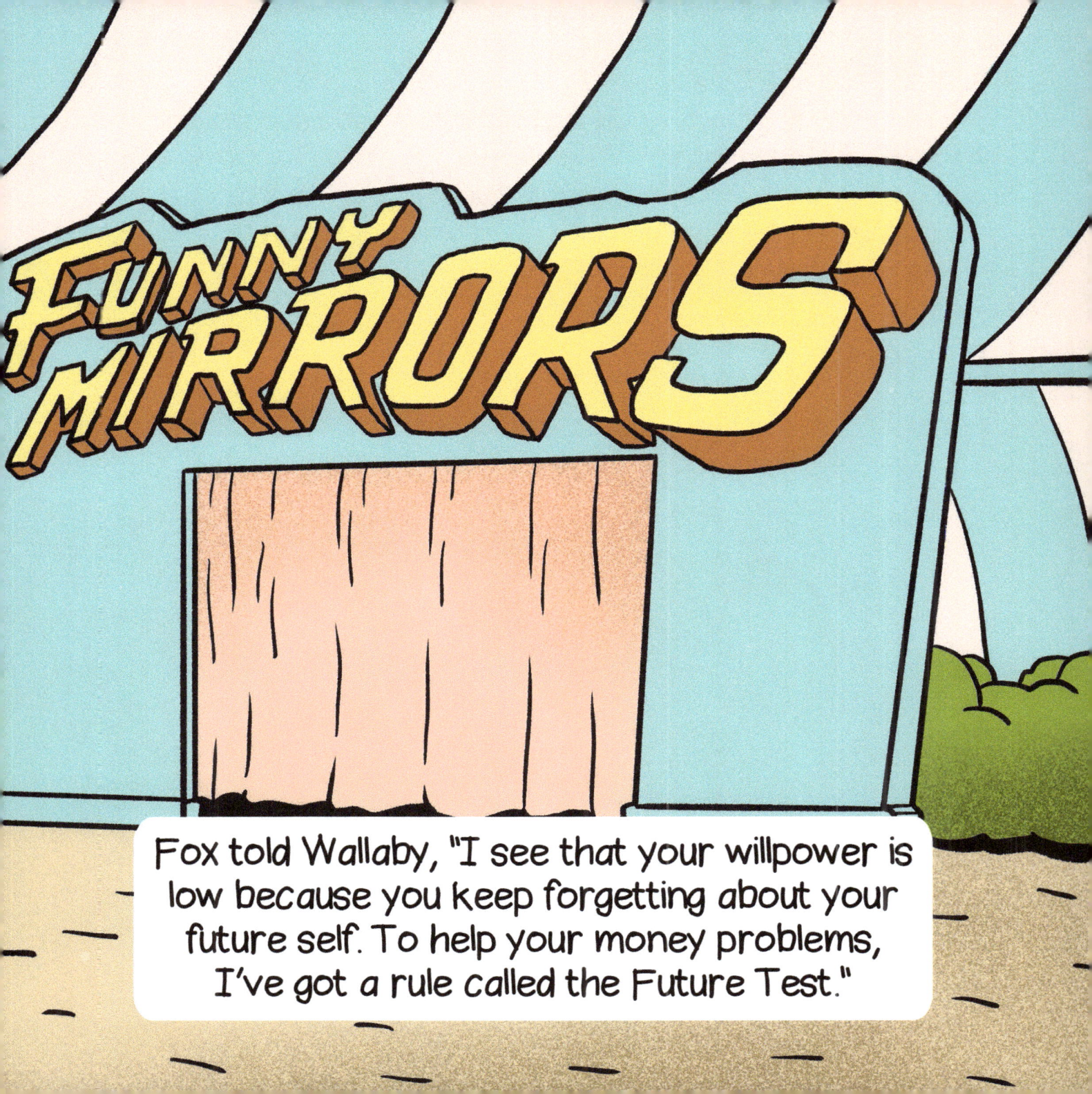

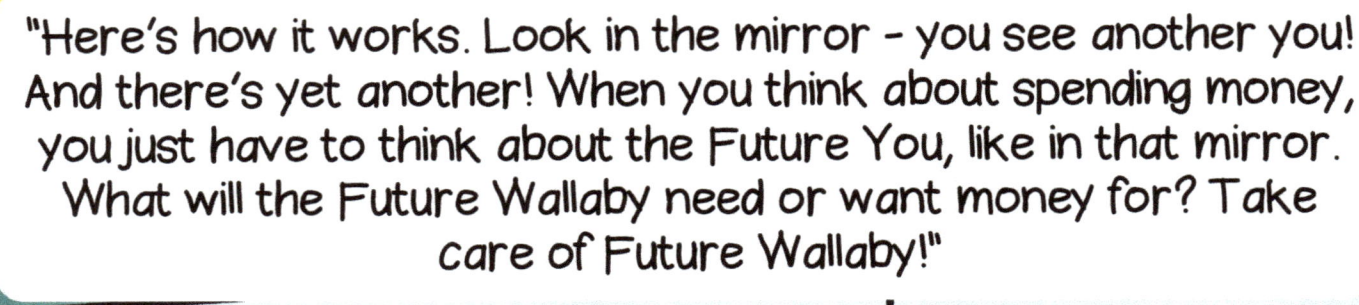

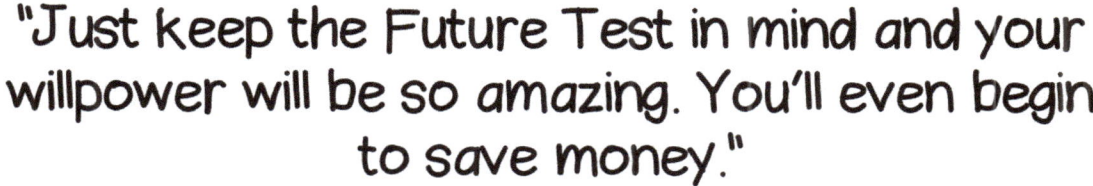

Wallaby was jumping for joy. He was so excited to try this out. Was willpower really as easy as looking in the mirror?

Wallaby was worried, of course. Change is never easy. But he knew that if you work hard enough, almost anything is possible.

Even though he wanted to order 5 hamburgers and 12 tacos, he knew Future Wallaby also needed to eat! So he only ordered 1 hamburger and 1 taco, and he still had lots of money for food later that week. Great!

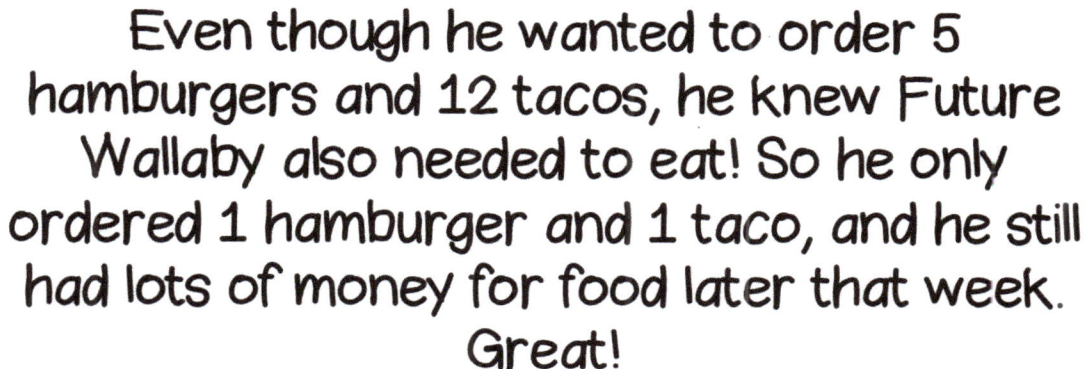